From Words To Wealth: Mastering Freelance Writing
By: Richard Krause

While every precaution has been taken in the preparation of this book, the publisher assumes no responsibility for errors or omissions, or for damages resulting from the use of the information contained herein.

FROM WORDS TO WEALTH: MASTERING FREELANCE WRITING

First edition. October 5, 2023.

Copyright © 2023 Richard Krause.

ISBN: 979-8223724865

Written by Richard Krause.

Also by Richard Krause

The Spice Cabinet Apothecary: Natural Health at Your Fingertips"
The Writer's Odyssey: Crafting Your Literary Legacy, A New Writer's
Guide Book
From Words To Wealth: Mastering Freelance Writing
The Morning Elixir of Life: The History and Art of Coffee

Watch for more at https://rkrause45.wixsite.com/mysite.

Foreword

In the digital age, the power of words has taken on a new significance. In a world where information is king, those who wield the pen skillfully hold the keys to success. Welcome to *"From Words to Wealth: Mastering Freelance Writing,"* your definitive guide to embarking on a journey that offers not just financial prosperity but the freedom to chart your own course.

Freelance writing is more than a profession; it's a gateway to unlimited opportunities. It's the art of transforming thoughts into words and words into wealth. Whether you're a budding wordsmith, a seasoned scribe, or someone simply intrigued by the idea of writing your way to financial freedom, this ebook is your passport to a realm where creativity meets prosperity.

We'll navigate the labyrinthine world of freelance writing together, uncovering the secrets to success that will empower you to:

◇ Discover your writing passion and unique voice.

◇ Master the essential writing skills that captivate audiences.

◇ Build a thriving freelance writing career from the comfort of your own home.

◇ Negotiate contracts and set rates that reflect your true worth.

⟡ Create a compelling writer's portfolio that opens doors to high-paying projects.

⟡ Forge lasting client relationships through effective communication and professionalism.

⟡ Navigate the ethical and legal nuances of freelance writing.

⟡ Diversify your income streams and expand your freelance business.

⟡ Find inspiration and overcome the challenges that every freelancer faces.

⟡ Embrace the future trends that will shape the freelance writing industry.

Join us on this exciting journey as we unveil the strategies, tips, and insights that will transform your words into wealth. Whether you're driven by the dream of financial independence or the love of the written word, "From Words to Wealth" is your guidebook to mastering freelance writing and crafting a life of both prosperity and creative fulfillment.

Are you ready to embark on your path to pen, profit, and freedom? Let's begin.

Chapter 1: Introduction to Freelance Writing

In the vast landscape of the digital age, where the hum of technology and the whisper of innovation reign supreme, there emerges a profession unlike any other—a profession that wields the power of words as its mightiest weapon. It's called freelance writing, a journey from the realms of thought to the realms of wealth. As we embark upon this odyssey of ink and imagination, we find ourselves at the threshold of an adventure that promises not only financial abundance but also the liberation to carve our own destiny.

Imagine, if you will, a world where your words are the architects of your success, where your sentences are the bridges that span the chasms between you and your dreams. This world is the domain of the freelance writer, where creativity and commerce intertwine in an intricate dance. In this first chapter, we step into the uncharted territory of freelance writing, where the very essence of words transforms into a key that unlocks the door to unparalleled prosperity.

The Freelance Writing Enigma

Freelance writing, it's a phrase that may echo through the corridors of your mind, familiar yet shrouded in mystery. To unravel this enigma, we must first understand its essence. At its core, freelance writing is the art of harnessing the written word to create content that informs, persuades, and delights. It's about crafting sentences that resonate with readers, that compel them to take action or simply savor the beauty of language.

In a world driven by content, freelance writers are the architects of ideas, the weavers of narratives, and the sculptors of information. They're the unseen hands behind the articles you read, the blogs you peruse, and the product descriptions that prompt you to click "Buy Now." They're the storytellers who breathe life into the digital realm, the educators who share knowledge, and the entertainers who whisk you away to new worlds—all through the power of words.

The Allure of Freelance Writing

But why venture into the realm of freelance writing? What makes it so irresistible to those who hear its siren call? The allure lies in the autonomy it bestows upon the writer. Imagine being the captain of your own literary ship, navigating the seas of creativity without the constraints of a 9-to-5 anchor. Picture working from the cozy confines of your own home, your fingers dancing across the keyboard as you weave words into a symphony of sentences.

For stay-at-home mothers, for individuals with disabilities, for those burdened by the shackles of hectic schedules, freelance writing offers the elixir of flexibility. You set your own hours, you march to the beat of your own writerly drum. Deadlines become your milestones, not your masters. It's a career path that aligns with life's twists and turns, a professional canvas where you paint your dreams.

And then, there's the promise of prosperity. In the world of freelance writing, your words are not just wisps of thought floating in the ether; they are tangible assets, assets that can earn you a handsome living. Imagine penning an eBook and receiving not just accolades but a paycheck of around $500. Yes, you heard that right—$500 for your words, for your thoughts, for your creation.

The Path Unfolds

Now, dear reader, you may wonder how one embarks upon this journey, how one treads the path from words to wealth. Fear not, for the path is illuminated with the wisdom and experiences of those who have trod upon it before you. In the chapters that follow, we will delve deep into the intricacies of freelance writing, exploring every nook and cranny of this wondrous world.

We shall unveil the secrets of finding your writing niche, of honing your skills to perfection, of setting up a haven of creativity within the confines of your home. We shall explore the labyrinth of freelance writing platforms and opportunities, guiding you through the maze of job listings and profiles. Contracts and negotiations will become your allies, and you'll emerge equipped with the art of deal-making.

But, my fellow wordsmith, we won't stop there. You shall learn the art of writing itself—how to craft content that not only informs but enchants, how to wield the sword of originality and the shield of meticulous proofreading. Your portfolio, like a treasure chest, shall store your finest literary gems, and your website will be the gallery where clients come to admire your craft.

With the passing of each chapter, we'll peel back the layers of the freelance writing onion, revealing the heart of a career built upon passion, perseverance, and precision. As we journey together, you'll uncover the secrets of managing your freelance career, from time management to client relations to financial acumen.

It won't always be smooth sailing. Challenges will rise like waves in the sea, but you'll learn to surf them with grace. Ethical dilemmas will test your mettle, but you'll emerge with your integrity intact. And when you reach the pinnacle of success, you'll find ways to scale your freelance empire and expand your horizons.

But before we get ahead of ourselves, dear reader, let us embark on this odyssey together. Let us tread the path from words to wealth, where the pen is indeed mightier than the sword, and where the allure of freelance writing is more than just a dream—it's a reality waiting to be written.

So, fasten your seatbelt and sharpen your pencils, for the adventure of a lifetime awaits. The world of freelance writing is calling your name, and "From Words to Wealth" is your map, your guide, and your key to unlocking the boundless possibilities that lie ahead.

Let's begin this enchanting journey, one word at a time.

Chapter 2: Discovering Your Freelance Writing Passion

In the realm of freelance writing, the journey begins not with a pen to paper, but with a question that echoes through the corridors of your mind: What do you truly love to write about? It is in this quest for passion, the spark that ignites the writer's soul, that we find the very foundation of a successful freelance writing career.

The Embrace of Passion

Picture a world where writing is not just a task, but a joy, a calling, a symphony of words flowing effortlessly from your mind to the page. This is the world we enter when we embrace our passion for writing. The act of putting pen to paper or fingers to keyboard becomes not a chore, but a dance—a dance of ideas, emotions, and creativity.

Passion is the compass that guides us through the vast wilderness of the writing landscape. It's the North Star that helps us navigate, ensuring that every word we write resonates with authenticity and purpose. It's the force that drives us to explore the depths of our chosen subjects, to unravel the mysteries of our niches, and to share our knowledge with the world.

Identifying Your Writing Interests

The journey to discovering your freelance writing passion begins with introspection. Take a moment to reflect on the topics that ignite a fire within you, the subjects that make your heart race and your mind come alive. Do you find yourself drawn to the world of technology, eager to explore the latest gadgets and innovations? Or does the world of travel beckon, with its promise of adventure and exploration?

Perhaps you're passionate about health and wellness, eager to share your insights on nutrition and fitness. Or maybe it's the realm of personal finance that piques your interest, with its opportunities to guide others toward financial prosperity. Whatever it may be, identifying your writing interests is the first step on this enchanting journey.

Finding Your Unique Writing Voice

As you embark on your freelance writing adventure, remember that your voice is your most valuable asset. Your voice is the fingerprint of your writing, the unique signature that sets you apart in a sea of words. It's the distinct tone, style, and perspective that make your writing unmistakably yours.

Discovering your unique writing voice is an exploration of self-expression. It's about embracing your individuality and allowing it to shine through your words. Are you a storyteller, weaving narratives that captivate readers? Are you a problem solver, offering practical solutions and guidance? Or are you a thought-provoker, challenging the status quo with your ideas and opinions?

Your voice is your superpower, and it's intricately linked to your passion. When you write about subjects that truly resonate with you, your voice becomes a beacon, drawing readers who share your enthusiasm and vision.

Why Passion Matters in Freelance Writing

Now, you may wonder, why is passion so vital in the world of freelance writing? The answer lies in the connection it fosters. When you write with passion, your words carry an authenticity that resonates with readers. Your enthusiasm becomes infectious, and your readers can sense the genuine interest you have in your chosen topics.

Passion also fuels your dedication. Freelance writing is not without its challenges, and there will be times when deadlines loom and writer's block threatens to stall your progress. It is during these moments that passion becomes your driving force. It's what compels you to push through obstacles, to keep writing even when the path seems arduous.

Moreover, passion leads to expertise. When you are deeply passionate about a subject, you naturally invest time in learning and exploring it. Your passion drives you to research, to stay up-to-date with the latest developments, and to continuously expand your knowledge. As a result, you become a trusted authority in your niche, a writer whose insights are sought after.

The Path Forward

As we conclude this chapter, let your heart and mind converge on the path ahead. In the world of freelance writing, passion is your compass, your guiding star. It's the foundation upon which your writing career is built. So, embrace your passions, identify your interests, and nurture your unique writing voice.

In the chapters that follow, we will delve deeper into the art of freelance writing, exploring the skills, strategies, and techniques that will empower you to transform your passions into compelling content. The journey has just begun, and the world of freelance writing awaits your unique voice, your boundless enthusiasm, and your unwavering dedication.

Prepare to embark on a voyage of words, where passion is your constant companion, and where every sentence you craft is a step closer to mastering the art of freelance writing.

Let your passions guide you, for the path from words to wealth is illuminated by the fire of your creativity and the brilliance of your words.

Chapter 3: Building Your Writing Foundation

In the world of freelance writing, the foundation upon which your writing prowess stands is akin to the bedrock of a towering skyscraper. It is the very ground from which your words spring forth, the canvas upon which your literary masterpiece is painted. As we delve into Chapter 3, we embark on the journey of building a formidable writing foundation, one that will empower you to craft compelling content that captures hearts and minds.

The Art of Effective Writing

Effective writing is the linchpin of the freelance writing craft. It's the art of conveying thoughts, ideas, and information in a way that engages, informs, and resonates with readers. The essence of effective writing lies in its ability to leave a lasting impression, to spark emotions, and to provoke thought.

At its core, effective writing is like a symphony, where words are the notes, and sentences are the melodies. It's about composing prose that flows seamlessly, where each word is a carefully chosen instrument in the orchestra of communication. Effective writing transcends the mundane and elevates words to the realm of art.

Grammar, Punctuation, and Style

To build a solid writing foundation, one must first master the tools of the trade. Grammar, like the scaffold of a grand structure, provides the framework upon which your sentences are constructed. It is the structure that ensures clarity and coherence in your writing. Proper grammar is the cornerstone of effective communication.

Punctuation, on the other hand, is the punctuation marks that add nuance and rhythm to your sentences. It's the commas that guide the reader's breath, the periods that signal the end of a thought, and the exclamation points that infuse excitement. Punctuation is the art of creating pauses and emphasis in your writing.

Style is the unique signature that sets your writing apart from the rest. It's the choice of words, the sentence structure, and the tone that give your writing its distinct flavor. Style is the brushstroke that paints a vivid picture in the reader's mind. It's what makes your writing unmistakably yours.

The Journey of Writing Proficiency

Building a strong writing foundation is not a sprint but a marathon. It's a journey of continuous learning and refinement. Just as a sculptor chisels away at a block of marble to reveal a masterpiece, so too must a writer hone their skills over time. Writing proficiency is the result of dedication, practice, and a commitment to improvement.

Begin your journey by embracing the basics of grammar and punctuation. Familiarize yourself with the rules and conventions of the English language. Learn how to construct sentences that are grammatically correct and coherent. Understand the subtle nuances of punctuation marks and how they affect the flow of your writing.

But proficiency goes beyond the mechanics of writing. It extends to the realm of storytelling, where you learn to craft narratives that captivate your audience. It encompasses the art of persuasion, where you wield words to influence and inspire. It includes the ability to adapt your writing style to different genres and audiences.

The Writer's Toolbox

As you embark on your quest for writing proficiency, consider the tools at your disposal. A writer's toolbox is filled with resources that can enhance your writing skills. Grammar and style guides, such as "The

Elements of Style" by Strunk and White, can be invaluable companions on your journey.

Writing exercises and prompts are like the training regimes of an athlete. They help you refine your skills, stretch your creativity, and overcome writer's block. Regular practice, in the form of daily writing, journaling, or blogging, is the crucible in which your writing abilities are forged.

Reading widely and voraciously is the sustenance that fuels your growth as a writer. It exposes you to different writing styles, voices, and genres. It introduces you to new ideas and perspectives. Reading is the nourishment that enriches your writing.

The Path Forward

As we conclude this chapter on building your writing foundation, envision your journey as that of a craftsman shaping a work of art. Your words are the raw materials, and your skills are the tools at your disposal. With each stroke of the pen or press of the keyboard, you chisel away at the marble of language, revealing the masterpiece within.

The path to writing proficiency is a continuous one, marked by dedication and a hunger for improvement. As you proceed in your journey, remember that every word you write, every sentence you craft, and every story you tell is a step toward mastery.

In the chapters that follow, we will delve deeper into the nuances of effective writing, exploring techniques, strategies, and exercises that will sharpen your skills. The world of freelance writing beckons, and it is your well-built writing foundation that will enable you to create content that captivates, informs, and inspires.

So, let your pen be your chisel, your keyboard your canvas, and your words your masterpiece. The journey to becoming a proficient writer is a path well worth treading, for it is the very essence of the freelance writing craft.

Chapter 4: Setting Up Your Freelance Writing Workspace

Imagine, if you will, a sanctuary of creativity, a realm where ideas flow freely, and words take flight like birds in the open sky. This is the realm of your freelance writing workspace—a place where the magic of words is conjured, where your thoughts find expression, and where your dreams take shape. In this chapter, we embark on the journey of creating a freelance writing haven, where inspiration and productivity intertwine.

The Power of Your Writing Environment

Before we delve into the practical aspects of setting up your freelance writing workspace, let's take a moment to appreciate the profound influence of your environment on your writing. Your workspace is not merely a physical location; it's a state of mind, a reservoir of inspiration.

Consider the great writers of history—Hemingway at his typewriter in the corner of a Parisian cafe, J.K. Rowling penning her wizarding tales in a cozy Edinburgh cafe. These writers understood the significance of their surroundings. Your workspace is where you craft the worlds you wish to share with your readers, and it should be a place that fosters creativity.

Designing a Productive Home Office

For many freelance writers, the home office is the canvas upon which their words take shape. It's a place of solitude and concentration, a sanctuary away from the distractions of daily life. Designing a productive home office requires thoughtful consideration of several key elements:

Location: Choose a location in your home that is quiet and free from interruptions. Consider factors such as natural light, access to power outlets, and proximity to amenities like a bathroom or kitchen.

Furniture: Invest in a comfortable chair and a sturdy desk. Your chair should provide support during long writing sessions, and your desk should have enough space for your computer, reference materials, and notepads.

Ergonomics: Pay attention to ergonomics to prevent physical strain. Your computer monitor should be at eye level, and your keyboard and mouse should be at a comfortable height. Use an ergonomic chair with lumbar support to maintain good posture.

Organization: Keep your workspace organized and clutter-free. Use shelves, drawers, or filing cabinets to store books, reference materials, and stationery. A clutter-free environment fosters mental clarity and focus.

Decoration: Personalize your workspace with items that inspire you. This could be artwork, quotes, or photographs. Surround yourself with objects that resonate with your creative spirit.

Essential Writing Tools and Software

A writer's tools are like a painter's brushes or a musician's instrument—they are the instruments of your craft. Equip your freelance writing workspace with the essential tools and software to enhance your writing efficiency:

Computer: Invest in a reliable computer with enough processing power and memory to handle your writing tasks. Consider a laptop for flexibility or a desktop for a dedicated workspace.

Word Processing Software: Choose a word processing software that suits your preferences. Microsoft Word, Google Docs, and Scrivener are popular options. These tools offer features like spell-check, grammar-check, and document formatting.

Reference Materials: Keep reference materials within reach. This could include style guides, dictionaries, thesauruses, and industry-specific books. Online resources like Grammarly and online dictionaries are also valuable.

Note-Taking Tools: Have notepads or digital note-taking apps available for jotting down ideas, outlines, and quick references. Tools like Evernote or OneNote are excellent for digital note-taking.

Writing Tools: Invest in quality pens, pencils, and notebooks for jotting down ideas and drafting outlines. Having tangible writing tools can be inspiring and practical.

Creating a Productive Work Routine

In your freelance writing workspace, routine is your ally. Establishing a productive work routine helps you manage your time efficiently and maintain focus. Here are some tips to consider:

Set Clear Work Hours: Establish specific work hours for your freelance writing. Define a start and end time for your workday to maintain a healthy work-life balance.

Create a To-Do List: Start your workday by creating a to-do list. Prioritize tasks and set goals for what you want to accomplish.

Breaks and Stretching: Take short breaks during your work hours to stretch, hydrate, and clear your mind. These breaks can boost your productivity and prevent burnout.

Minimize Distractions: Identify potential distractions in your workspace and take steps to minimize them. Turn off social media notifications, silence your phone, and close unrelated browser tabs.

Stay Organized: Keep your workspace organized and tidy. Organizational tools like calendars and task management apps can help you stay on top of deadlines and projects.

The Path Forward

As we conclude this chapter on setting up your freelance writing workspace, envision it as your creative cocoon, your sanctuary of inspiration. Your workspace is where the magic of your words comes to life, where your thoughts find their voice, and where your dreams take flight.

In the chapters that follow, we will delve deeper into the practical aspects of freelance writing, from finding opportunities and negotiating contracts to crafting compelling content. Your well-designed workspace is the launch pad from which you'll embark on your freelance writing journey.

So, let your freelance writing workspace be a reflection of your creativity and a testament to your commitment. Design it with care, equip it with the tools of your trade, and infuse it with the inspiration that fuels your words.

As you write and create in this space, remember that it's more than just a physical location; it's the crucible in which your ideas evolve into eloquent prose. Let your workspace be your partner in the wondrous journey from words to wealth.

Chapter 5: The Freelance Writing Market Landscape

In the ever-expanding universe of freelance writing, the landscape is both vast and intricate. It resembles a bustling marketplace, where writers, clients, and opportunities converge. As we embark on Chapter 5, we navigate the terrain of the freelance writing market—a realm where demand and supply, niches and specialties, and opportunities and challenges intertwine.

The Ecosystem of Freelance Writing

Before we delve into the dynamics of the freelance writing market, let's envision it as a thriving ecosystem. At its heart are writers, each a unique species with its own set of skills, interests, and styles. These writers, like the diverse flora and fauna of an ecosystem, play distinct roles in the freelance writing landscape.

Clients, on the other hand, are akin to the ecosystem's inhabitants—each seeking specific services, be it articles, blog posts, web content, or eBooks. They are the lifeblood of the freelance writing world, providing the nutrients that sustain writers. Their needs, preferences, and budgets vary, creating niches and specialties within the ecosystem.

Understanding Market Demand

Central to the freelance writing market is the concept of demand. It's the heartbeat that drives the ecosystem forward. Demand in the freelance writing world is not static; it ebbs and flows with the tides of the digital age. Understanding market demand is akin to reading the seasons of an ecosystem.

Demand can be influenced by a multitude of factors, including industry trends, current events, and emerging technologies. For example, during a global health crisis, there may be a surge in demand for health-related content. In the same vein, advancements in technology can lead to a demand for articles on the latest gadgets or software.

Exploring Different Freelance Writing Niches

Within the freelance writing market, niches are the specialized habitats where writers thrive. A niche is like a microcosm within the larger ecosystem, characterized by its unique set of topics, audiences, and writing styles. Exploring different niches is akin to studying the diverse ecosystems found across the planet.

Consider the myriad niches in freelance writing:

1. **Health and Wellness**: Writers in this niche may focus on topics like nutrition, fitness, mental health, or medical advancements.

2. **Technology**: This niche encompasses everything from gadgets and software reviews to articles on emerging technologies like artificial intelligence and blockchain.

3. **Travel and Lifestyle**: Travel writers explore destinations, cultures, and experiences, while lifestyle writers delve into topics like fashion, home decor, and personal development.

4. **Finance and Business**: Writers in this niche cover topics ranging from personal finance and investing to entrepreneurship and corporate finance.

5. **Education**: Educational writers create content for e-learning platforms, textbooks, and educational websites, covering subjects from mathematics to history.

Each niche has its unique characteristics, audience expectations, and opportunities for writers. Writers often choose niches based on their interests, expertise, and market demand.

Researching Profitable Writing Opportunities

In the freelance writing market, opportunity is the currency that writers seek. But how does one discover these opportunities? The answer lies in research. Research is akin to exploring uncharted territories, mapping out potential paths to success.

To uncover profitable writing opportunities, consider the following strategies:

Market Research: Investigate the current trends and demands within your chosen niche. What topics are popular? What keywords are trending? Tools like Google Trends and keyword research tools can be invaluable.

Competitor Analysis: Study the work of successful writers in your niche. What types of content do they produce? How do they engage with their audience? Learn from their strategies and tactics.

Client Needs: Understand your potential clients. What type of content do they require? What are their pain points and goals? Tailor your services to meet their needs.

Networking: Build relationships within the freelance writing community. Networking with fellow writers and industry professionals can lead to referrals and collaborations.

The Path Forward

As we conclude this chapter on the freelance writing market landscape, envision it as a vibrant ecosystem teeming with life and opportunity. The freelance writing market is not a static entity but a dynamic and evolving one, shaped by the ever-changing demands and preferences of clients and readers alike.

In the chapters that follow, we will delve deeper into the practical aspects of freelance writing, from crafting a compelling portfolio and finding opportunities on freelance platforms to negotiating rates and delivering exceptional work. Your understanding of the freelance writing market will serve as a compass, guiding you toward the most promising opportunities.

Prepare to embark on a journey through the heart of the freelance writing market, where writers and clients converge, where niches are explored, and where opportunities are waiting to be seized. The freelance writing world is a vast and intricate ecosystem, and with the right knowledge and skills, you can navigate its terrain and thrive within its diverse niches.

So, let curiosity be your guide, and let your passion for writing illuminate your path through the labyrinthine landscape of the freelance writing market. As you explore the niches, understand the demands, and seize the opportunities, you'll be well on your way to mastering the art of freelance writing.

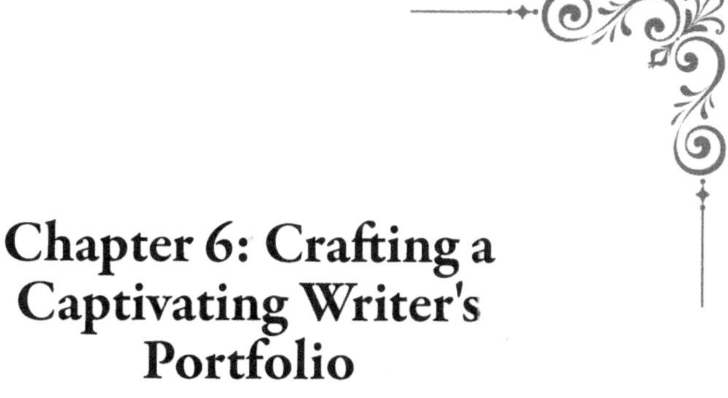

Chapter 6: Crafting a Captivating Writer's Portfolio

I magine a treasure chest filled with gems of your own creation—each gem a testament to your skill, your creativity, and your unique voice. This treasure chest is your writer's portfolio, a collection of your best work that dazzles potential clients and opens doors to freelance writing opportunities. In this chapter, we delve into the art of crafting a captivating writer's portfolio, a showcase of your talent that leaves a lasting impression.

THE PORTFOLIO'S ROLE in Freelance Writing

Before we delve into the nitty-gritty of portfolio creation, let's understand why it holds such significance in the freelance writing world. Think of your portfolio as the map that leads clients to your buried treasure—the treasure being your writing skills and expertise.

Your portfolio serves several essential functions:

1. **Demonstrating Your Skills**: It provides concrete evidence of your writing abilities, showcasing your mastery of grammar, style, and storytelling.

2. **Showcasing Your Range**: A well-rounded portfolio displays your versatility as a writer. It illustrates your ability to tackle diverse topics, styles, and formats.

3. **Building Trust**: A professional portfolio instills confidence in potential clients. It demonstrates that you are a serious and experienced writer.

4. **Setting Expectations**: Your portfolio sets the expectations for the quality of work clients can anticipate. It's your chance to make a compelling first impression.

Selecting Your Portfolio Pieces

Now, let's delve into the art of selecting the right pieces for your writer's portfolio—a task akin to curating a gallery exhibition. Your portfolio should represent the best of your work, offering a glimpse into your writing prowess. Here's how to make those selections:

1. **Quality Over Quantity**: Choose pieces that exemplify your best work. It's better to have a smaller number of high-quality samples than a large collection of mediocre ones.

2. **Variety Matters**: Include samples that showcase your versatility. If you can write in different styles (e.g., informative, persuasive, narrative), demonstrate this range in your portfolio.

3. **Highlight Expertise**: If you have expertise in a particular niche (e.g., technology, health, finance), prioritize including samples related to that niche. Clients often seek writers with subject matter knowledge.

4. **Freshness Counts**: Select recent pieces that reflect your current skills and style. The writing landscape evolves, and your portfolio should reflect your up-to-date abilities.

5. **Diversity of Formats**: Include samples in various formats, such as blog posts, articles, case studies, or eBooks, to show that you can adapt to different types of writing.

6. **Client Success Stories**: If you have received positive feedback or testimonials from clients, consider including them alongside the relevant portfolio pieces.

Formatting Your Portfolio

Your writer's portfolio is not just about the content; it's also about the presentation. Think of it as the display case that showcases your literary treasures. Here are some formatting tips:

1. **Professional Website**: If possible, create a professional website to host your portfolio. A personal domain (e.g., www.yourname.com[1]) adds an extra layer of professionalism.

2. **Clear Organization**: Organize your portfolio logically, with categories or sections for different niches or writing styles. Make it easy for visitors to navigate.

3. **Engaging Introductions**: Accompany each portfolio piece with a brief introduction that provides context for the work. Explain the client, the purpose, and your role in creating it.

4. **Visual Appeal**: Use clean and visually appealing design. Incorporate images, graphics, or multimedia elements when relevant. Ensure that your portfolio is mobile-friendly.

---

1. http://www.yourname.com/

5. **Call to Action**: Include a clear call to action, such as a "Hire Me" button or contact information, so potential clients know how to reach you.

6. **Regular Updates**: Keep your portfolio up-to-date by adding new pieces and removing outdated ones. A stale portfolio can give the impression of inactivity.

Creating a Compelling About Page

In addition to your portfolio pieces, your writer's website should have an "About" page. This page is your chance to introduce yourself to potential clients and build a personal connection. Here's what to include:

1. **Your Story**: Share a bit about your background, your writing journey, and what led you to freelance writing. Make it relatable and engaging.

2. **Your Expertise**: Highlight your areas of expertise and any unique qualifications or experiences that set you apart as a writer.

3. **Client Testimonials**: If you have received positive feedback from clients, feature some testimonials on your About page to build trust.

4. **Your Approach**: Explain your approach to writing—your commitment to quality, your dedication to meeting deadlines, and your passion for delivering results.

5. **Contact Information**: Provide clear contact information or a contact form so that potential clients can easily reach out to you.

The Path Forward

As we conclude this chapter on crafting a captivating writer's portfolio, envision it as your literary exhibit—an exquisite collection of your finest work. Your portfolio is your passport to freelance writing opportunities, a showcase of your talent that beckons clients to collaborate with you.

In the chapters that follow, we will delve deeper into the practical aspects of freelance writing, from finding clients and negotiating rates to delivering exceptional work and managing your freelance business. Your well-crafted portfolio is the gateway to these opportunities.

Prepare to embark on a journey where your words are your most precious treasures, where your portfolio is your guide, and where your talent shines brightly. The freelance writing world awaits, and with a compelling writer's portfolio, you're poised to make a memorable entrance.

So, let your portfolio tell your story, showcase your skills, and leave a lasting impression. Craft it with care, curate it with your best work, and let it be a beacon that draws clients to your unique talents as a freelance writer.

Chapter 7: Finding Freelance Writing Opportunities

Imagine the freelance writing world as a vast treasure map, with opportunities scattered like hidden gems waiting to be unearthed. In this chapter, we embark on a quest to discover these opportunities—a journey that takes us from the well-trodden paths of online job boards to the uncharted territories of networking and self-marketing. As we navigate this terrain, you will uncover the secrets to finding freelance writing opportunities that align with your skills and aspirations.

The Multifaceted Landscape of Opportunities

The freelance writing world is a multifaceted landscape, with opportunities that span a spectrum of possibilities. Whether you're just starting your writing journey or seeking to expand your horizons, there are diverse avenues to explore:

1. **Online Job Boards**: Think of these as bustling marketplaces where clients post writing projects and freelancers bid on them. Popular platforms include Upwork, Freelancer, and Fiverr.

2. **Content Mills**: These are platforms that connect writers with clients in need of content. While they often offer lower

rates, they can be a good starting point for beginners. Examples include Textbroker and iWriter.

3. **Content Agencies**: Content agencies hire freelance writers to produce content for their clients. These agencies can provide a steady stream of work. Look for agencies specializing in your niche.

4. **Pitching to Publications**: Consider submitting pitches to magazines, newspapers, and online publications that accept freelance contributions. Research their guidelines and target your pitches accordingly.

5. **Self-Publishing**: If you're interested in creative writing, consider self-publishing your books or eBooks through platforms like Amazon Kindle Direct Publishing (KDP).

6. **Blogging and Guest Posting**: Start your own blog or contribute guest posts to established blogs in your niche. This can help showcase your expertise and attract clients.

7. **Networking**: Building relationships within the writing community can lead to referrals and direct opportunities. Attend writing conferences, join online forums, and engage with fellow writers.

8. **Self-Marketing**: Create a professional writer's website to showcase your portfolio and services. Use social media and online forums to establish your presence as a writer.

Navigating Online Job Boards

Online job boards are a popular starting point for many freelance writers. These platforms offer a wide range of writing opportunities, from one-time gigs to long-term projects. To navigate them effectively, consider these tips:

1. **Complete Your Profile**: Create a detailed and professional profile that highlights your skills, experience, and expertise. Use a clear profile picture and write a compelling bio.

2. **Search Smartly**: Use specific keywords and filters to narrow down job searches to your niche or preferred type of writing.

3. **Write Persuasive Proposals**: Craft custom proposals for each job you apply to. Address the client's needs and explain why you're the right fit for the project.

4. **Build a Strong Portfolio**: Your portfolio is your showcase. Regularly update it with your best work to make a strong impression on potential clients.

5. **Set Realistic Rates**: Research the going rates for freelance writing in your niche and region. Be competitive but also ensure you're paid what you're worth.

6. **Communicate Effectively**: Promptly respond to messages and inquiries from clients. Professional communication is key to building trust.

Pitching to Publications

If you have a passion for journalism or creative non-fiction, consider pitching your ideas to publications. Here's how to get started:

1. **Research Publications**: Identify magazines, newspapers, and online publications that align with your interests and

expertise. Study their guidelines and submission requirements.

2. **Craft Engaging Pitches**: Write compelling pitch emails that concisely outline your idea, its relevance, and your qualifications to write it.

3. **Follow Up**: Don't be discouraged by rejection. Editors receive numerous pitches daily. A polite follow-up email can sometimes lead to reconsideration.

4. **Build Relationships**: Cultivate relationships with editors by delivering high-quality work and meeting deadlines. A positive track record can lead to repeat assignments.

Networking and Self-Marketing

Building a network and marketing your services as a writer can open doors to freelance opportunities. Here are strategies to consider:

1. **Attend Writing Events**: Participate in writing conferences, workshops, and seminars. These events offer opportunities to connect with fellow writers, editors, and potential clients.

2. **Join Online Communities**: Engage in online forums, social media groups, and platforms like LinkedIn where writers and clients gather. Share your insights, ask questions, and offer assistance.

3. **Create a Writer's Website**: Develop a professional website that showcases your portfolio, services, and contact information. A well-optimized website can attract clients via online searches.

4. **Guest Blogging**: Contribute guest posts to authoritative blogs in your niche. This not only establishes your expertise but can also lead to client inquiries.

5. **Freelance Directly**: If you identify potential clients or businesses that could benefit from your services, reach out to them directly with a well-crafted proposal.

The Path Forward

As we conclude this chapter on finding freelance writing opportunities, envision it as the beginning of your quest—a journey filled with potential and discovery. The freelance writing landscape is diverse, offering numerous pathways to explore.

In the chapters that follow, we will delve deeper into the practical aspects of freelance writing, from negotiating rates and delivering exceptional work to managing your freelance business and expanding your career. Your ability to find and seize opportunities will serve as the compass guiding you through this terrain.

Prepare to embark on a journey where your writing talents are your greatest treasures, where opportunity awaits around every corner, and where your passion for words propels you forward. The freelance writing world is vast, but with the right strategies and determination, you can uncover the gems hidden within its terrain.

Let curiosity be your guide, and let your persistence be your torch as you navigate the intricate map of freelance writing opportunities. As you explore, connect, and market your skills, you'll discover that the path to success in this dynamic field is rich with possibilities.

Chapter 8: Negotiating Rates and Contracts

In the realm of freelance writing, where words are currency and ideas hold value, negotiations become the bridge between your talent and your livelihood. As we embark on Chapter 8, we delve into the art of negotiating rates and contracts—a journey through the intricate dance of securing fair compensation, protecting your rights, and nurturing lasting client relationships.

Understanding the Value of Your Work

Before stepping onto the negotiation stage, it's crucial to understand the inherent value of your work. Your words have the power to inform, persuade, entertain, and inspire. They are the building blocks of content that capture attention, engage readers, and drive action. Recognize that your skills as a writer are the cornerstone of effective communication.

To determine the value of your work, consider the following factors:

1. **Expertise**: Your level of expertise in a particular niche or writing style can command higher rates. Specialized knowledge adds value to your content.

2. **Research**: Content that requires extensive research or in-depth analysis often merits higher compensation. Research-intensive projects demand time and effort.

3. **Complexity**: The complexity of the writing task influences its value. Technical, scientific, or highly specialized content may command higher rates.

4. **Audience**: Writing for a niche or industry with a limited audience may require a premium due to the specialized knowledge needed.

5. **Revisions**: Factor in the number of revisions included in the contract. Additional revisions beyond the agreed-upon scope may warrant extra compensation.

Setting Your Rates

Setting your freelance writing rates is a delicate balancing act. You want to secure fair compensation for your work without pricing yourself out of the market. Consider these strategies when determining your rates:

1. **Market Research**: Investigate the going rates for freelance writing in your niche and region. Online resources, industry surveys, and freelance writing forums can provide valuable insights.

2. **Hourly vs. Per-Word vs. Project-Based**: Decide whether you'll charge per hour, per word, or on a project-based fee structure. Each has its merits and considerations.

3. **Consider Expenses**: Account for overhead expenses such as taxes, software, research materials, and marketing efforts when calculating your rates.

4. **Experience and Expertise**: As your experience and expertise grow, you can gradually increase your rates to reflect your improved skills and reputation.

5. **Negotiation Room**: Be prepared for negotiations. It's common for clients to request adjustments to your rates, so decide in advance how flexible you're willing to be.

Creating a Clear Contract

A well-drafted contract is the foundation of a successful freelance writing project. It defines the scope of work, expectations, timelines, and compensation terms. A contract not only protects your interests but also fosters transparency and trust with your clients. Here's what to include:

1. **Scope of Work**: Clearly outline the specific writing tasks, word count, format, and any additional deliverables (e.g., revisions, research) in the contract.

2. **Timelines**: Specify project milestones, deadlines, and the schedule for deliverables. This ensures everyone is on the same page regarding project timelines.

3. **Compensation**: Detail the compensation structure, including rates, payment schedule, and any additional fees or expenses. Be explicit about payment methods and terms.

4. **Rights and Ownership**: Define who owns the rights to the content. Many freelance contracts grant the client full rights upon payment, while others may allow the writer to retain certain rights.

5. **Revisions and Edits**: Clarify the number of revisions or edits included in the contract. Specify how additional revisions will be handled and whether they incur extra charges.

6. **Confidentiality and Non-Disclosure**: If necessary, include clauses regarding confidentiality and non-disclosure of sensitive information.

7. **Termination Clause**: Outline the circumstances under which either party can terminate the contract and the procedures to follow.

8. **Dispute Resolution**: Include a clause specifying how disputes will be resolved, whether through arbitration, mediation, or other means.

9. **Signatures**: Both you and the client should sign the contract to indicate your agreement. Electronic signatures are legally binding and convenient.

Effective Negotiation Strategies

Effective negotiation is an art that requires finesse and preparation. Here are some strategies to employ during the negotiation process:

1. **Prepare Thoroughly**: Familiarize yourself with the project, the client's needs, and your own value as a writer before entering negotiations.

2. **Listen Actively**: Pay close attention to the client's needs and expectations. Listening is as crucial as speaking during negotiations.

3. **Be Flexible**: While it's important to know your worth, be open to compromise. Consider the overall value of the project beyond just the monetary compensation.

4. **Stay Professional**: Maintain a professional and courteous demeanor throughout negotiations. A positive rapport is valuable for future collaborations.

5. **Use Written Communication**: Whenever possible, conduct negotiations in writing. This provides a record of agreements and ensures clarity.

6. **Don't Rush**: Take your time with negotiations. Avoid making hasty decisions or concessions. Sometimes, a pause for reflection can lead to a better outcome.

The Path Forward

As we conclude this chapter on negotiating rates and contracts, envision it as the refining fire that molds your freelance writing career. Negotiations are not merely transactions but the building blocks of trust, collaboration, and long-term success.

In the chapters that follow, we will delve deeper into the practical aspects of freelance writing, from delivering exceptional work and managing client relationships to growing your freelance business and navigating challenges. Your ability to negotiate rates and contracts will serve as a compass guiding you through these varied landscapes.

Prepare to embark on a journey where your words hold value, where your expertise is recognized, and where your negotiation skills enable you to forge mutually beneficial partnerships. The world of freelance writing is shaped by these intricate negotiations, and with each successful agreement, you're one step closer to mastering the art of freelance writing.

Chapter 9: Delivering Exceptional Work

In the realm of freelance writing, the ink-stained canvas awaits the artist's touch, and the blank page yearns for the writer's words. As we embark on Chapter 9, we delve into the sacred art of delivering exceptional work—an exploration of the craft and dedication required to transform ideas into eloquent prose that captivates, informs, and inspires.

The Essence of Exceptional Writing

Exceptional writing is like a finely tuned instrument—its melodies resonate with readers, leaving a lasting impression. But what defines exceptional writing? It's a harmonious blend of several essential elements:

1. **Clarity**: Exceptional writing is crystal clear. It conveys ideas without ambiguity or confusion. It guides readers effortlessly through the narrative.

2. **Engagement**: It captivates and immerses readers, making them eager to journey through the text. Exceptional writing sparks curiosity and maintains interest.

3. **Relevance**: It addresses the needs and interests of the target audience. It offers valuable insights, answers questions, or entertains in a meaningful way.

4. **Originality**: Exceptional writing is unique and fresh. It offers a perspective or insight that distinguishes it from the mundane.

5. **Empathy**: It resonates with readers on an emotional level, evoking empathy, laughter, or contemplation.

The Writing Process

The path to exceptional writing begins with a systematic approach—a journey through the phases of ideation, creation, refinement, and delivery. Let's explore these stages:

1. **Ideation**: This is the inception of your writing journey. It involves brainstorming ideas, conducting research, and defining your objectives. Identify the purpose of your piece: Is it to inform, persuade, entertain, or inspire?

2. **Research**: Research is the foundation of exceptional writing. It provides the knowledge and facts that lend authority and depth to your content. Thorough research ensures accuracy and credibility.

3. **Planning**: Before putting pen to paper, outline your structure. A well-organized plan serves as your roadmap, ensuring your writing flows logically and cohesively.

4. **Drafting**: Begin writing your first draft. Don't fret about perfection at this stage; focus on getting your ideas on paper. Allow your creativity to flow freely.

5. **Revision**: Revision is where exceptional writing takes shape. Review your work critically, assessing clarity, coherence, and relevance. Edit for grammar, spelling, and style.

6. **Proofreading**: After revision, proofread meticulously. Pay attention to punctuation, grammar, and typos. A polished piece reflects professionalism.

7. **Seek Feedback**: Don't hesitate to seek feedback from peers, mentors, or editors. Fresh perspectives can uncover blind spots and refine your work.

8. **Final Review**: Conduct a final review to ensure your content aligns with your objectives and meets the needs of your audience.

Crafting Captivating Introductions and Conclusions

The introduction and conclusion are the bookends of your writing, and they wield immense power in shaping the reader's experience.

Introduction: A captivating introduction beckons readers into your world of words. Consider these techniques:

1. **Anecdote**: Start with a compelling story or anecdote that relates to your topic.

2. **Question**: Pose a thought-provoking question that piques curiosity.

3. **Statistical Insight**: Use a surprising statistic or fact that highlights the importance of your topic.

4. **Quote**: Begin with a relevant and insightful quote from a notable figure.

5. **Thesis Statement**: Clearly state the purpose of your piece to provide direction.

Conclusion: The conclusion leaves a lasting impression. It should tie together your ideas and provide closure. Consider these techniques:

1. **Summarize Key Points**: Briefly recap the main points of your piece.

2. **Call to Action**: If appropriate, encourage readers to take action or consider a specific viewpoint.

3. **End with Impact**: Conclude with a powerful statement, question, or reflection that lingers in the reader's mind.

Meeting Client Expectations

For freelance writers, delivering exceptional work often means meeting or exceeding client expectations. Effective communication with clients is paramount. Here's how to ensure alignment:

1. **Clarify Expectations**: At the outset, establish a clear understanding of the project scope, goals, and client expectations. Discuss the target audience and style preferences.

2. **Set Milestones**: If the project is extensive, consider setting milestones to keep both you and the client on track.

3. **Timely Updates**: Provide regular updates on your progress. Communication builds trust and transparency.

4. **Address Feedback**: Be open to client feedback and revisions. A willingness to adapt shows your commitment to delivering quality work.

5. **Meet Deadlines**: Meeting deadlines is non-negotiable. Reliability is a hallmark of professionalism.

NURTURING CLIENT RELATIONSHIPS

Exceptional writers not only produce outstanding work but also cultivate lasting client relationships. Consider these strategies:

1. **Professionalism**: Maintain professionalism in all interactions. Promptly respond to emails, meet deadlines, and communicate clearly.

2. **Appreciation**: Express gratitude for your clients' business. A simple thank-you note can go a long way.

3. **Exceed Expectations**: Whenever possible, go the extra mile. Surprise clients with work that exceeds their expectations.

4. **Feedback Loop**: Encourage clients to provide feedback, not only on the final product but also on your collaboration process.

5. **Long-Term Value**: Look beyond individual projects. Consider how you can provide ongoing value to your clients and become their go-to writer.

The Path Forward

As we conclude this chapter on delivering exceptional work, envision it as a masterful stroke on the canvas of your freelance writing career. Exceptional writing isn't a destination but an ongoing journey of refinement and dedication.

In the chapters that follow, we will delve deeper into the practical aspects of freelance writing, from managing your freelance business and navigating challenges to expanding your career and thriving in this dynamic field. Your ability to consistently deliver exceptional work will serve as your beacon in this writer's odyssey.

Prepare to embark on a journey where your words are your legacy, where your dedication fuels your craft, and where your commitment to excellence elevates you to new heights as a freelance writer. Exceptional writing is not an elusive dream; it's the tapestry you weave with every keystroke, the legacy you leave with every published piece.

Chapter 10: Freelance Writing Challenges and Triumphs

In the labyrinthine world of freelance writing, the path to success is not without its twists, turns, and challenges. Yet, within this intricate journey lie opportunities for triumph and growth. As we delve into Chapter 10, we navigate the terrain of freelance writing's challenges and celebrate the triumphs that await those who persevere.

THE CHALLENGE OF REJECTION

Rejection is a formidable adversary that every freelance writer encounters. It comes in many forms: a rejected pitch, an unresponsive client, or a manuscript returned with extensive edits. In these moments, it's easy to feel disheartened, but remember, rejection is not a verdict on your worth as a writer.

Triumph: Triumph over rejection by viewing it as a stepping stone to improvement. Each rejection holds valuable lessons. Analyze feedback, refine your approach, and persevere with newfound wisdom.

The Battle with Writer's Block

Writer's block, that insidious foe, can strike without warning, leaving you staring at a blank screen, bereft of words. It's a common challenge, but one that can be conquered.

Triumph: Triumph over writer's block by adopting strategies to rekindle your creativity. Take a break, change your environment, or write freely without judgment. Remember that even in the darkest block, a spark of inspiration can ignite.

Balancing Act: Time Management

The freelance writer's life offers the allure of flexibility, but it also presents the challenge of self-discipline. Balancing multiple projects, meeting deadlines, and managing time effectively can be a daunting task.

Triumph: Triumph over time management challenges by creating a structured schedule. Set clear work hours, establish priorities, and use time management tools to stay organized. Remember, effective time management can lead to greater productivity.

Client Relations and Communication Hurdles

Effective communication with clients is crucial, but misunderstandings can occur. Whether it's misaligned expectations, unclear project scope, or disputes over revisions, navigating client relations can be challenging.

Triumph: Triumph over communication hurdles by fostering open and transparent communication. Seek clarity on project details, expectations, and deadlines from the outset. Document agreements in writing to mitigate misunderstandings. A constructive dialogue can often resolve issues.

Financial Uncertainties

Freelance writing offers financial independence, but it can also bring financial uncertainty. Irregular income, managing taxes, and financial planning can be daunting tasks.

Triumph: Triumph over financial uncertainties by creating a financial plan. Set aside a portion of your income for taxes, establish an emergency fund, and consider diversifying your income streams through multiple clients or passive income opportunities. Financial stability is attainable with foresight and discipline.

Staying Inspired and Motivated

The allure of freelance writing can wane when the novelty fades and motivation dwindles. Keeping the creative fires burning and staying inspired is an ongoing challenge.

Triumph: Triumph over waning motivation by nurturing your creative spirit. Find inspiration in diverse sources—books, art, nature, or conversations. Set goals and celebrate milestones to keep your enthusiasm alive. Remember, passion is a renewable resource.

Expanding Your Skillset

The world of writing is ever-evolving, and freelance writers must adapt to changing trends and technologies. The challenge lies in continuously expanding your skillset to stay competitive.

Triumph: Triumph over the challenge of skill development by committing to lifelong learning. Take online courses, read industry blogs, and explore new writing styles. Embrace change as an opportunity to evolve and grow as a writer.

Navigating Freelance Marketplaces

Freelance marketplaces can be a double-edged sword. While they offer opportunities, they also present challenges such as stiff competition and potential low-paying gigs.

Triumph: Triumph over marketplace challenges by strategically positioning yourself. Build a compelling portfolio, seek niche markets, and target clients who value quality work. Over time, you can transition from low-paying gigs to higher-paying opportunities.

The Rewards of Resilience

In the tumultuous journey of freelance writing, resilience is your steadfast companion. The challenges you face are the crucibles in which your skills are honed, your character is tested, and your determination is forged.

With each challenge you conquer, you emerge stronger, wiser, and more resilient. The triumphs that follow are not just achievements; they are testament to your unwavering commitment to the craft of writing.

THE PATH FORWARD

As we conclude this chapter on freelance writing challenges and triumphs, envision it as the crucible that shapes your mettle as a writer. Challenges are not roadblocks but opportunities to elevate your craft and redefine your limits.

In the chapters that follow, we will delve deeper into the practical aspects of freelance writing, from expanding your career and establishing your presence to thriving in the ever-evolving landscape of writing. Your ability to face challenges head-on and emerge triumphant will serve as the compass guiding you through these uncharted territories.

Prepare to embark on a journey where challenges are your catalysts for growth, where triumphs are your laurels of accomplishment, and where your passion for writing propels you forward. The world of freelance writing is shaped by those who dare to confront challenges and emerge victorious, and you are poised to be among them.

Chapter 11: Establishing Your Writing Presence

In the vast expanse of the digital realm, establishing your writing presence is akin to carving your name into the annals of the literary world. As we delve into Chapter 11, we embark on a journey to create a distinct and influential presence as a freelance writer—a voyage through the intricacies of branding, online platforms, and building an audience that hangs on your every word.

The Power of Branding

In a world awash with content, branding sets you apart as a writer. Your brand is the essence of who you are, what you stand for, and the promise you make to your audience. Crafting a compelling brand identity is the cornerstone of establishing your writing presence.

Brand Identity: Define your unique brand identity. Consider your writing style, values, and niche expertise. Your brand should resonate with your target audience.

Brand Name: Choose a name that encapsulates your brand. It may be your own name or a pseudonym that aligns with your writing persona.

Logo and Visuals: Develop a logo and visual elements that represent your brand. Consistency in design across your online presence reinforces brand recognition.

Mission Statement: Craft a concise mission statement that encapsulates your writing goals and what readers can expect from your work.

Online Platforms: Your Digital Showcase

In the digital age, online platforms serve as your showcase to the world. These platforms are where you exhibit your writing prowess, engage with your audience, and amplify your voice.

Website: A professional website is your online home. It serves as the hub of your writing presence, showcasing your portfolio, blog, and contact information. Ensure it's user-friendly and visually appealing.

Social Media: Social media platforms are invaluable for connecting with readers. Choose platforms that align with your target audience. Regularly share your work, engage with comments, and nurture your online community.

Writing Portfolios: Maintain an up-to-date writing portfolio that highlights your best work. Showcase a diverse range of writing styles and topics to demonstrate your versatility.

Blogging: A blog offers a platform to share your insights, opinions, and expertise. Consistent and high-quality blog posts can attract readers and establish your authority in your niche.

Email Newsletter: Build an email list to connect directly with your readers. Share exclusive content, updates, and insights. An engaged email list can be a powerful asset.

Audience Engagement: Building Your Tribe

Your audience is not just a passive readership; they are your community, your tribe. Engaging with your audience fosters loyalty, trust, and lasting connections.

Respond Promptly: Acknowledge comments, messages, and emails from your readers. Prompt responses show that you value their input.

Interact Authentically: Be authentic in your interactions. Share personal insights, anecdotes, and experiences to create a genuine connection.

Ask for Feedback: Encourage readers to provide feedback on your work. Their insights can guide your future content and strengthen your relationship.

Collaborate: Collaborate with fellow writers, bloggers, and influencers. Joint ventures and guest posts can expand your reach and introduce your writing to new audiences.

Consistency Is Key

Consistency is the bedrock of establishing your writing presence. Whether it's in your posting schedule, tone, or engagement with readers, consistency builds trust and reliability.

Posting Schedule: Maintain a consistent posting schedule for your blog and social media. Regularity keeps your audience engaged and returning for more.

Voice and Style: Develop a consistent voice and writing style. It becomes your signature, instantly recognizable to your readers.

Branding Elements: Use consistent branding elements, such as your logo, color palette, and tagline, across all platforms to reinforce your identity.

Networking: Expanding Your Reach

Networking is the conduit through which you expand your writing presence. It's about forging connections, sharing insights, and collaborating with others in your field.

Writing Communities: Join online writing communities, forums, and social media groups. Engage in discussions, share your expertise, and seek advice from fellow writers.

Conferences and Events: Attend writing conferences, webinars, and literary events. Networking at such events can lead to valuable connections and opportunities.

Guest Posting: Contribute guest posts to authoritative blogs and publications in your niche. This not only expands your reach but also establishes your authority.

Interviews and Podcasts: Participate in interviews or podcasts related to your niche. These platforms can introduce you to new audiences and establish your expertise.

The Path Forward

As we conclude this chapter on establishing your writing presence, envision it as the gateway to a vibrant and influential career as a freelance writer. Your presence is not just your online footprint; it's your legacy, your voice in the digital cacophony.

In the chapters that follow, we will delve deeper into the practical aspects of freelance writing, from thriving in the industry and managing your business to honing your skills and achieving your writing aspirations. Your ability to establish a captivating writing presence will serve as the guiding star in this ever-evolving digital universe.

Prepare to embark on a journey where your writing presence leaves an indelible mark, where your words resonate far and wide, and where your influence as a writer extends beyond the screen. The digital realm awaits, and you are poised to shape it with the power of your writing presence.

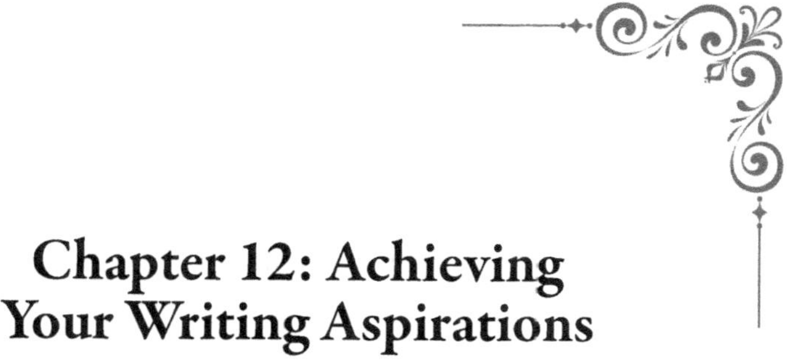

Chapter 12: Achieving Your Writing Aspirations

In the labyrinth of freelance writing, where words are both your compass and your canvas, the pursuit of your writing aspirations becomes a guiding star. As we embark on Chapter 12, we delve into the realm of dreams and ambitions—the tapestry of goals, growth, and the realization of your deepest writing desires.

The Power of Aspirations

Writing aspirations are the seeds of your creative journey. They define your goals, inspire your efforts, and shape your path as a writer. Embracing your aspirations empowers you to reach new heights and evolve as a freelance writer.

Dream Big: Your aspirations should be audacious. Dare to dream big, for it is in the grandest dreams that you often find the greatest motivation.

Clarity of Purpose: Define your writing aspirations with clarity. What do you wish to achieve? Is it publishing a novel, becoming a renowned blogger, or winning prestigious awards?

Short-Term and Long-Term Goals: Break down your aspirations into short-term and long-term goals. Short-term goals provide immediate direction, while long-term goals chart your overarching vision.

Setting SMART Goals: SMART goals are Specific, Measurable, Achievable, Relevant, and Time-bound. They provide a structured framework for pursuing your aspirations.

Continuous Learning and Growth

The journey to achieving your writing aspirations is also a journey of continuous learning and growth. It's a testament to your commitment to honing your craft and expanding your horizons.

Online Courses and Workshops: Enroll in online writing courses, workshops, and seminars to acquire new skills and perspectives. Lifelong learning is the key to progress.

Reading Widely: Read voraciously and diversify your literary diet. Explore genres and authors outside your comfort zone to broaden your creative palette.

Mentorship: Seek mentorship from experienced writers who can offer guidance, feedback, and insights. Their wisdom can accelerate your growth.

Join Writing Groups: Join writing groups or critique circles to connect with peers. Sharing your work and receiving constructive feedback fosters improvement.

Persistence in the Face of Challenges

The path to achieving your writing aspirations is seldom without obstacles. Challenges may arise, but your persistence and resilience will carry you through.

Rejection and Criticism: Expect rejection and criticism along the way. These are not setbacks but opportunities for growth and refinement.

Embrace Failure: Embrace failure as a stepping stone to success. Many accomplished writers faced rejection before achieving acclaim.

Adaptability: Be adaptable and open to change. The writing landscape is dynamic, and the ability to pivot and evolve is a valuable asset.

The Role of Self-Belief

Self-belief is the cornerstone of pursuing your writing aspirations. It's the unshakable faith in your abilities and the unwavering conviction that your dreams are attainable.

Overcoming Self-Doubt: Acknowledge moments of self-doubt, but do not let them deter you. Celebrate your accomplishments and remember your capabilities.

Visualize Success: Visualize yourself achieving your writing aspirations. This mental exercise can bolster your confidence and motivation.

Positive Affirmations: Use positive affirmations to boost your self-belief. Repeat affirmations that reinforce your faith in your writing journey.

Building a Support System

Behind every successful writer is a support system that offers encouragement, feedback, and a safety net during challenging times.

Family and Friends: Share your writing aspirations with your loved ones. Their support can provide emotional strength and motivation.

Writing Communities: Engage with writing communities and forums. These spaces offer camaraderie, advice, and shared experiences with fellow writers.

Accountability Partners: Consider having an accountability partner—a fellow writer with whom you share goals and progress updates. Mutual support can keep you on track.

Celebrating Milestones

Celebrate your achievements, both big and small, along your writing journey. Each milestone reached is a testament to your dedication and progress.

Create Milestone Markers: Set milestone markers for your writing aspirations. Celebrate completing a manuscript, hitting a certain word count, or publishing an article.

Reward Yourself: Treat yourself when you achieve a goal. Whether it's a small indulgence or a meaningful reward, acknowledgment of your efforts is essential.

Reflect and Reset: Periodically reflect on your progress and adjust your goals if necessary. As you grow, your aspirations may evolve, and that's perfectly normal.

The Path Forward

As we conclude this chapter on achieving your writing aspirations, envision it as the summit reached after a long and arduous climb. Your aspirations are not just distant dreams; they are your destiny, your purpose as a writer.

In the chapters that follow, we will delve deeper into the practical aspects of freelance writing, from thriving in the industry and managing your business to refining your skills and expanding your horizons. Your pursuit of your writing aspirations will serve as the guiding star in this expansive galaxy of words.

Prepare to embark on a journey where your aspirations fuel your creativity, where your determination drives your progress, and where your dreams of becoming an accomplished writer become a vibrant reality. The world of freelance writing is shaped by those who dare to aspire and are unyielding in their pursuit, and you are poised to be among them.

Chapter 13: Expanding Your Freelance Writing Career

As the journey of your freelance writing career unfolds, you find yourself at the precipice of expansion—a realm where new horizons beckon, and your capabilities as a writer are primed for growth. In Chapter 13, we delve into the art of expanding your freelance writing career—an odyssey through diversification, scaling up, and venturing into uncharted territories.

The Impetus for Expansion

Expansion is not merely a choice; it's often a necessity in the evolving landscape of freelance writing. There are several driving forces that propel writers to explore new avenues and broaden their horizons.

Diversifying Income: Relying solely on one client or income stream can be precarious. Diversification mitigates risks and provides stability.

Professional Growth: Expanding your career allows you to cultivate new skills, learn from different experiences, and stay engaged and passionate about your work.

Meeting Market Demands: As market demands change, expanding into new niches or services ensures that you remain relevant and adaptable.

Scaling Your Business: For those aiming to build a freelance writing business, expansion is the key to scaling up operations and increasing revenue.

Diversification of Services

Diversification is the cornerstone of expansion. It involves broadening the array of writing services you offer, allowing you to cater to a wider range of clients and projects.

Content Types: Consider diversifying into different content types such as blog posts, whitepapers, case studies, social media content, or video scripts.

Niche Specialization: Explore various niches or industries that align with your interests and expertise. Niche specialization can command higher rates.

Additional Services: Offer complementary services such as editing, proofreading, SEO optimization, or content strategy. These services enhance your value.

Targeting Different Clients: Expand your client base by targeting diverse client profiles, from startups to established corporations, nonprofits to educational institutions.

Scaling Your Workload

As you expand your freelance writing career, managing an increased workload becomes paramount. Effective strategies are essential for maintaining quality and preventing burnout.

Time Management: Implement time management techniques, such as the Pomodoro Technique or time-blocking, to maximize productivity.

Outsourcing: Consider outsourcing tasks like research, editing, or administrative work to freelancers or virtual assistants.

Automation: Utilize automation tools for tasks like social media posting, email marketing, or project management to streamline operations.

Setting Boundaries: Establish clear boundaries regarding working hours and client expectations to prevent over committing.

Building Your Brand

Expanding your freelance writing career also means fortifying your brand presence. A strong brand not only attracts clients but also reinforces your credibility.

Rebranding: If your brand no longer aligns with your expanded services or target audience, consider rebranding to reflect your new identity.

Updating Portfolio: Regularly update your writing portfolio to showcase your diversified services and the quality of your work.

Content Marketing: Implement a content marketing strategy that demonstrates your expertise in your chosen niches and services.

Networking: Engage with professionals in your expanded niches through networking events, conferences, and online communities.

Venturing into New Territories

Expansion often involves venturing into uncharted territories. This may entail exploring new writing styles, industries, or content formats.

Experimental Writing: Embrace experimental writing styles, whether it's creative nonfiction, poetry, or immersive storytelling. These ventures can enhance your creativity and portfolio.

Emerging Industries: Keep an eye on emerging industries and trends. Being an early adopter can position you as an expert in a burgeoning field.

International Markets: Expand into international markets by offering content in multiple languages or catering to a global audience.

Evolving Technology: Embrace technological advancements such as interactive content, virtual reality, or artificial intelligence-driven writing tools.

Staying Adaptable

Adaptability is the linchpin of successful expansion. In the ever-changing landscape of freelance writing, the ability to pivot and evolve is a valuable asset.

Market Research: Continuously conduct market research to identify emerging trends, client needs, and competitive landscapes.

Learning Agility: Stay committed to lifelong learning. Acquire new skills, stay updated on industry best practices, and be open to change.

Feedback Loop: Seek feedback from clients and peers. Feedback provides insights for improvement and helps you adapt to changing client preferences.

Measuring Success

Expansion should not be arbitrary. Define your goals and metrics for success, so you can gauge the impact of your endeavors.

Key Performance Indicators (KPIs): Establish KPIs that align with your expansion goals. These could include revenue growth, client retention rates, or portfolio diversity.

Regular Evaluation: Periodically evaluate the effectiveness of your expansion strategies. Adjust your approach based on performance.

Celebrating Achievements: Celebrate milestones and achievements along your expansion journey. Recognizing progress fuels motivation.

The Path Forward

As we conclude this chapter on expanding your freelance writing career, envision it as the voyage of a seasoned explorer, charting new territories on a boundless map of possibilities. Your expansion is not just about venturing into the unknown; it's about evolving into the writer you aspire to be.

In the chapters that follow, we will delve deeper into the practical aspects of freelance writing, from managing your business and honing your skills to thriving in a dynamic industry and shaping your writing legacy. Your expansion is the compass that guides you through these uncharted waters of the writing world.

Prepare to embark on a journey where expansion is your compass, where versatility is your strength, and where your freelance writing career flourishes in the ever-expanding universe of words. The world of freelance writing is shaped by those who dare to explore and adapt, and you are poised to be among them.

Chapter 14: Thriving in the Dynamic World of Writing

The dynamic world of writing is akin to a churning sea, constantly shifting and reshaping itself. Thriving in this tumultuous terrain requires more than mere survival—it demands adaptability, resilience, and a commitment to excellence. In Chapter 14, we embark on a journey to explore the art of thriving as a freelance writer—a voyage through innovation, self-care, and the enduring pursuit of writing mastery.

Embracing Innovation

In the ever-evolving landscape of writing, innovation is your compass. It's about exploring new horizons, embracing technology, and staying at the forefront of industry trends.

Tech Integration: Integrate technology into your writing process. Explore writing apps, AI-assisted tools, and digital platforms that enhance productivity and creativity.

Interactive Content: Experiment with interactive content formats such as quizzes, polls, and infographics. Engaging content captivates readers and sets you apart.

Video and Podcasting: Venture into video content or podcasting. These multimedia formats can expand your audience and provide new storytelling avenues.

Embracing Change: Be open to change and adapt swiftly to emerging trends. A willingness to evolve keeps your writing fresh and relevant.

The Art of Self-Care

Thriving as a freelance writer necessitates taking care of your most vital asset—you. Self-care is not a luxury but a necessity for longevity and creativity.

Balance: Maintain a work-life balance. Allocate time for leisure, family, and personal interests to prevent burnout.

Physical Health: Prioritize physical health with regular exercise, a balanced diet, and sufficient sleep. A healthy body fosters a sharp mind.

Mental Well-being: Nurture your mental well-being. Practice mindfulness, seek support when needed, and manage stress to sustain creativity.

Setting Boundaries: Establish boundaries with clients and colleagues. Respect for your time and space is essential for self-care.

The Pursuit of Mastery

Thriving as a freelance writer involves the relentless pursuit of mastery—a commitment to refining your craft, expanding your knowledge, and honing your skills.

Continuous Learning: Stay hungry for knowledge. Enroll in courses, attend workshops, and read widely to stay updated on industry trends and writing techniques.

Feedback Loop: Seek constructive feedback on your work. Peer reviews, writing groups, and client input offer valuable insights for improvement.

Portfolio Enhancement: Regularly update and enhance your portfolio. Showcase your best work to demonstrate your growth and expertise.

Writing Challenges: Participate in writing challenges, competitions, or collaborations. These experiences stretch your abilities and inspire innovation.

Navigating the Gig Economy

Thriving in the gig economy requires strategic navigation. As a freelance writer, you must adapt to the nuances of short-term contracts, project-based work, and variable income.

Financial Planning: Implement a robust financial plan. Save for taxes, create an emergency fund, and manage your income to account for lean periods.

Multiple Income Streams: Diversify your income sources. Explore affiliate marketing, online courses, or content licensing to supplement your freelance earnings.

Client Relations: Cultivate strong client relationships. Deliver exceptional service, communicate effectively, and seek long-term collaborations.

Networking: Continue to expand your professional network. Connections can lead to new opportunities and provide support during challenging times.

The Legacy of Words

Thriving as a freelance writer is not merely about the present—it's about crafting a lasting legacy through your words. Your writing has the power to inspire, inform, and influence generations.

Impactful Writing: Strive to create writing that leaves an impact. Whether it's through storytelling, thought leadership, or advocacy, aim to make a difference.

Authenticity: Infuse authenticity into your work. Authentic writing resonates with readers and leaves an indelible impression.

Legacy Projects: Consider undertaking legacy projects. These are works of passion and significance that define your writer's journey.

Mentorship: Pay it forward by mentoring aspiring writers. Your guidance can shape the next generation of wordsmiths.

The Path Forward

As we conclude this chapter on thriving in the dynamic world of writing, envision it as the culmination of your journey—a tapestry woven with innovation, self-care, mastery, and a profound appreciation for the enduring power of words.

In the chapters that follow, we will delve deeper into the practical aspects of freelance writing, from managing your business and marketing your services to perfecting your craft and achieving your aspirations. Your ability to thrive in the dynamic world of writing will be your guiding light as you navigate the uncharted waters of the writing realm.

Prepare to embark on a journey where thriving is not just a goal but a way of life, where adaptability is your greatest asset, and where your writing legacy endures through the ages. The world of freelance writing is shaped by those who dare to thrive amidst the chaos, and you are poised to be among them.

Chapter 15: Shaping Your Writing Legacy

As your journey through the intricate world of freelance writing nears its culmination, you stand on the precipice of something extraordinary—a legacy crafted from the indomitable spirit of your words. In Chapter 15, we embark on a profound exploration of shaping your writing legacy—an odyssey through reflection, contribution, and the enduring impact of your craft.

The Essence of a Writing Legacy

A writing legacy is not a mere footnote in history; it's an eternal echo of your thoughts, emotions, and experiences captured in words. It transcends time, inspiring generations and leaving an indelible mark on the literary tapestry.

Reflection: Begin by reflecting on your writing journey. What themes, stories, or ideas have consistently resonated in your work? What message or emotion do you want your legacy to convey?

Defining Moments: Identify defining moments in your career—the pieces of writing that encapsulate your voice and vision. These become the foundation of your legacy.

Contributing to Culture

A writing legacy is intertwined with the cultural fabric of society. Your words have the power to influence, educate, and spark change.

Social Commentary: Consider addressing pressing social issues through your writing. Thoughtful commentary can shed light on important topics and ignite conversations.

Education: Share your knowledge and experiences. Write articles, guides, or books that educate and empower readers, contributing to their personal growth.

Inspiration: Inspire others through your stories, achievements, and resilience. Your journey as a freelance writer can motivate aspiring writers to pursue their dreams.

CAPTURING MOMENTS IN Time

Writing has the unique ability to capture moments in time, preserving them for posterity. Your legacy can serve as a time capsule, transporting readers to different eras and experiences.

Historical Narratives: Explore historical narratives through your writing. Whether it's memoirs, historical fiction, or in-depth research, your work can offer glimpses into the past.

Personal Chronicles: Document your own life experiences and observations. Personal essays and reflections can provide a window into the human condition.

Cultural Significance: Write about cultural events, traditions, or customs that hold significance. Your work can help preserve cultural heritage.

The Craft of Writing Mastery

To shape a lasting legacy, mastery of the craft is essential. Commit to refining your writing skills, experimenting with new styles, and continually pushing the boundaries of your creativity.

Innovative Techniques: Experiment with innovative writing techniques. From stream-of-consciousness to nonlinear storytelling, innovation adds depth to your legacy.

Voice and Style: Hone your unique voice and style. These distinct qualities define your legacy and make your writing instantly recognizable.

Literary Influence: Pay homage to literary influences that have shaped your writing. Acknowledging your mentors and inspirations is a way to honor their contributions.

Teaching and Mentorship

A profound aspect of shaping a writing legacy is passing on your knowledge and wisdom to aspiring writers. Mentorship and teaching become pivotal.

Mentoring: Take on mentees and guide them on their writing journeys. Your mentorship can have a profound impact on their growth and success.

Teaching: Consider teaching writing classes or workshops. Sharing your expertise with others enriches the writing community and extends your influence.

Legacy Projects: Embark on legacy projects, such as writing guides, books, or courses, specifically designed to impart your knowledge and insights.

The Legacy Beyond Words

A writing legacy extends beyond the written word. It encompasses the lives you touch, the conversations you inspire, and the change you effect.

Community Engagement: Engage with your writing community. Participate in discussions, support fellow writers, and contribute to the growth of the literary world.

Advocacy: Use your writing platform for advocacy. Champion causes you are passionate about and leverage your influence to drive positive change.

Influence on Others: Acknowledge the impact your writing has on others. Encourage readers and fellow writers to share their own stories and insights.

The Path Forward

As we conclude this chapter on shaping your writing legacy, envision it as the pinnacle of your journey—an eloquent testimony to your dedication, creativity, and the profound influence of your words.

In the chapters that follow, we will delve deeper into the practical aspects of freelance writing, from managing your business and marketing your services to perfecting your craft and achieving your aspirations. Your legacy is not just a destination; it's an ongoing journey of refinement and dedication.

Prepare to embark on a journey where your words are your legacy, where your dedication fuels your craft, and where your commitment to excellence elevates you to new heights as a freelance writer. Exceptional writing is not an elusive dream; it's the tapestry you weave with every keystroke, the legacy you leave with every published piece.

Chapter 16: Navigating the Business of Freelance Writing

As you journey deeper into the world of freelance writing, you encounter a critical facet of your craft—the business side of it all. In Chapter 16, we embark on an exploration of navigating the intricate landscape of the business of freelance writing—a voyage through entrepreneurship, client relationships, financial acumen, and the path to sustainable success.

The Freelance Writing Business

Freelance writing is not just an art; it's also a business. Embracing this dual role is essential for long-term success.

Entrepreneurial Mindset: Adopt an entrepreneurial mindset. View yourself as a business owner and your writing as a valuable product or service.

Business Plan: Develop a business plan that outlines your goals, target audience, pricing strategy, and marketing approach. A plan provides direction and accountability.

Legal Considerations: Familiarize yourself with the legal aspects of freelance writing. Contracts, copyrights, and taxes are critical components of your business.

Financial Management

Sound financial management is the cornerstone of a sustainable freelance writing career. It involves budgeting, saving, and planning for both short-term and long-term financial goals.

Budgeting: Create a detailed budget that accounts for both personal and business expenses. Tracking your finances helps you maintain control.

Emergency Fund: Build an emergency fund to cushion against financial uncertainties. Aim for at least three to six months' worth of living expenses.

Retirement Planning: Plan for retirement by exploring retirement accounts such as IRAs or SEP-IRAs. Freelancers lack employer-sponsored plans, making self-funded retirement crucial.

Pricing Your Services

Determining your pricing structure is a crucial aspect of the freelance writing business. Striking the right balance between competitive rates and fair compensation is key.

Market Research: Conduct market research to understand prevailing rates for freelance writing services in your niche. This information informs your pricing strategy.

Hourly vs. Project-Based: Decide whether to charge hourly or offer project-based rates. Project-based rates provide transparency and predictability for both you and your clients.

Value-Based Pricing: Consider value-based pricing, where you price your services based on the perceived value they offer to the client. This approach can lead to higher earnings.

Client Relationships

Building strong client relationships is a linchpin of freelance success. Clients who trust and value your work are more likely to provide repeat business and referrals.

Communication: Maintain open and clear communication with clients. Regular updates, timely responses, and a professional demeanor foster trust.

Expectation Setting: Set clear expectations with clients regarding project scope, deadlines, and deliverables. Managing expectations prevents misunderstandings.

Client Feedback: Encourage clients to provide feedback on your work. Constructive criticism helps you improve and demonstrates your commitment to quality.

Marketing Your Services

Effective marketing is vital for attracting new clients and maintaining a steady flow of projects.

Online Presence: Maintain a professional online presence through a website and social media profiles. Showcase your portfolio, client testimonials, and contact information.

Networking: Network with fellow writers, editors, and professionals in your niche. Networking events, conferences, and online communities can lead to valuable connections.

Content Marketing: Use content marketing to showcase your expertise. Blogging, guest posting, and content creation establish your authority in your niche.

Sustainable Growth

Sustainability is not just about environmental conservation—it applies to your freelance writing business too. Sustainable growth ensures your business thrives over the long term.

Client Diversity: Diversify your client base to mitigate risk. Relying on a single client or industry can make your business vulnerable to economic fluctuations.

Work-Life Balance: Maintain a healthy work-life balance. Overworking can lead to burnout, affecting your productivity and the quality of your work.

Professional Development: Invest in your professional development. Attend workshops, take courses, and stay updated on industry trends to remain competitive.

The Path Forward

As we conclude this chapter on navigating the business of freelance writing, envision it as the fusion of your creative and entrepreneurial spirit. Your business acumen complements your writing prowess, enabling you to not only craft compelling content but also build a sustainable and prosperous career.

In the chapters that follow, we will delve deeper into the practical aspects of freelance writing, from perfecting your craft and marketing your services to achieving your aspirations and leaving a lasting legacy. Your business skills will serve as the compass that guides you through the intricacies of the freelance writing world.

Prepare to embark on a journey where creativity meets commerce, where your writing business thrives, and where your passion for words fuels your entrepreneurial spirit. The world of freelance writing is shaped by those who master the art of writing and the science of business, and you are poised to be among them.

Chapter 17: Achieving Your Freelance Writing Aspirations

As you traverse the intricate landscape of freelance writing, the culmination of your journey draws near. In Chapter 17, we embark on an exhilarating exploration of how to achieve your freelance writing aspirations—an odyssey through goal-setting, perseverance, and the unwavering pursuit of your dreams.

The Power of Aspirations

Freelance writing aspirations are the North Star guiding your creative journey. They are not mere dreams; they are the fuel propelling you toward your writing destiny.

Vision Clarity: Begin by defining your aspirations with crystalline clarity. What do you seek to achieve in your writing career? Is it publishing a novel, launching a successful blog, or becoming an influential industry voice?

Short-Term and Long-Term Goals: Break down your aspirations into manageable short-term and long-term goals. Short-term goals provide immediate direction, while long-term goals are the pillars of your overarching vision.

SMART Goals: SMART goals are Specific, Measurable, Achievable, Relevant, and Time-bound. Craft your aspirations into SMART goals, offering a structured path forward.

Continuous Learning and Growth

To realize your freelance writing aspirations, you must be committed to perpetual growth and learning. The journey to mastery is continuous.

Online Courses and Workshops: Enroll in online writing courses and workshops to acquire new skills and insights. Lifelong learning is the key to progress.

Widening Literary Horizons: Read extensively and diversify your literary diet. Exploring genres and authors beyond your comfort zone enriches your creative palette.

Mentorship: Seek guidance and mentorship from experienced writers. Their wisdom can accelerate your growth and provide valuable feedback.

Joining Writing Communities: Engage with writing communities and critique circles. Sharing your work and receiving constructive feedback nurtures improvement.

Persistence in the Face of Challenges

As you strive for your freelance writing aspirations, challenges are inevitable. These obstacles are not roadblocks but stepping stones on your path to success.

Rejection and Criticism: Expect rejection and criticism in your journey. These experiences are not setbacks but opportunities for growth and refinement.

Embrace Failure: Embrace failure as a teacher. Many accomplished writers faced rejection before achieving their goals. Each setback is a lesson.

Adaptability: Be adaptable and open to change. The writing landscape is dynamic, and the ability to pivot and evolve is a valuable asset.

The Role of Self-Belief

Self-belief is the bedrock of pursuing your freelance writing aspirations. It's the unwavering faith in your abilities and the conviction that your dreams are attainable.

Overcoming Self-Doubt: Acknowledge moments of self-doubt, but do not let them deter you. Celebrate your achievements and remember your capabilities.

Visualize Success: Cultivate a habit of visualizing yourself achieving your writing aspirations. This mental exercise can bolster your confidence and motivation.

Positive Affirmations: Harness the power of positive affirmations. Repeatedly affirm your belief in your writing journey and the realization of your aspirations.

Building a Support System

Behind every successful writer is a support system that offers encouragement, feedback, and a safety net during challenging times.

Family and Friends: Share your writing aspirations with your loved ones. Their support provides emotional strength and motivation.

Writing Communities: Engage with writing communities and forums. These spaces offer camaraderie, advice, and shared experiences with fellow writers.

Accountability Partners: Consider having an accountability partner—a fellow writer with whom you share goals and progress updates. Mutual support keeps you on track.

Celebrating Milestones

Celebrate your accomplishments, both big and small, along your writing journey. Each milestone reached is a testament to your dedication and progress.

Create Milestone Markers: Set tangible milestone markers for your writing aspirations. Celebrate completing a manuscript, hitting a word count goal, or publishing an article.

Reward Yourself: Treat yourself when you achieve a goal. Whether it's a small indulgence or a meaningful reward, acknowledgment of your efforts is essential.

Reflect and Reset: Periodically reflect on your progress and adjust your goals if necessary. As you grow, your aspirations may evolve, and that's perfectly normal.

The Path Forward

As we conclude this chapter on achieving your freelance writing aspirations, envision it as the summit reached after a long and arduous climb. Your aspirations are not just distant dreams; they are your destiny, your purpose as a writer.

In the chapters that follow, we will delve deeper into the practical aspects of freelance writing, from thriving in the industry and managing your business to refining your skills and expanding your horizons. Your pursuit of your writing aspirations will serve as the guiding star in this expansive galaxy of words.

Prepare to embark on a journey where your aspirations fuel your creativity, your determination drives your progress, and your dreams of becoming an accomplished writer become a vibrant reality. The world of freelance writing is shaped by those who dare to aspire and are unyielding in their pursuit, and you are poised to be among them.

Chapter 18: Embracing the Writer's Life

The writer's life is a distinctive and captivating journey, filled with the ebb and flow of creativity, the tapestry of words, and the ever-present allure of the blank page. In Chapter 18, we embark on an exploration of what it truly means to embrace the writer's life—an odyssey through the writer's routine, creative rituals, writer's block, and the intrinsic connection between life and art.

The Daily Ritual of a Writer

For a writer, routine is more than just a schedule; it's a sacred ritual. The rhythm of your day sets the stage for the creative act.

Morning Inspiration: Some writers find their muse in the quiet of the morning, with a fresh cup of coffee or tea. The dawn hours offer a serene canvas for creative exploration.

Midday Solitude: Others thrive in the hustle and bustle of midday. A bustling café, a library corner, or a park bench becomes their writing sanctuary.

Nighttime Reverie: Night owls revel in the stillness of the night. The world sleeps, and their imagination awakens, weaving stories under the moon's watchful gaze.

The Writing Space: Your writing space is your creative cocoon. Whether it's a cluttered desk, a cozy nook, or a sunlit garden, it's where ideas take shape.

Creative Rituals

Writers often rely on creative rituals to invoke inspiration and overcome the blank page's intimidation.

Journaling: Some writers begin with journaling, pouring their thoughts onto paper as a warm-up exercise before diving into their work.

Inspiration Boards: Others create inspiration boards adorned with images, quotes, and snippets that kindle their creative fire.

Music or Silence: The choice between music and silence is pivotal. Some writers find solace in instrumental melodies, while others prefer the symphony of silence.

The Struggle with Writer's Block

Writer's block is an adversary every writer faces at some point. It's the enigmatic force that dams the flow of words. Conquering it is an art.

Writing Prompts: Writing prompts are like keys that unlock creativity. They offer a spark, a direction, and a lifeline when you're stranded in the desert of writer's block.

Freewriting: Freewriting is a liberation exercise. Set a timer, write whatever comes to mind without inhibition, and let the words flow without judgment.

Change of Scenery: A change of scenery often breaks the shackles of writer's block. Take a walk, visit a museum, or simply step outside to breathe fresh air.

The Intersection of Life and Art

Life and art are intertwined. Your experiences, emotions, and observations become the raw material for your writing.

Life's Imprint: Life leaves its imprint on your writing. Every heartache, joy, struggle, and triumph finds its way into your words, making them resonate with authenticity.

Emotional Catharsis: Writing is catharsis. It's the medium through which you process your emotions, heal your wounds, and celebrate your victories.

Observational Skills: A writer is an eternal observer. You notice the subtlest details—the way sunlight filters through leaves, the fleeting expressions on strangers' faces, and the rhythm of conversations.

The Writer's Evolution

The writer's life is a journey of evolution. With each word written, each story told, and each book published, you grow and transform.

Exploring Genres: Don't confine yourself to a single genre. Explore different forms of writing—fiction, nonfiction, poetry, essays—and discover where your voice shines.

Voice Development: Your writing voice is not static; it matures with time and practice. Embrace the evolution, but also honor the essence that remains constant.

Author Brand: As you evolve, your author brand evolves too. Consider how your identity as a writer aligns with your work and resonates with your readers.

The Writer's Legacy

Every writer aspires to leave behind a legacy—a body of work that lingers in the minds and hearts of readers.

Timelessness: Seek timelessness in your writing. Craft stories and essays that transcend eras and resonate with generations.

Impact: Your writing has the power to impact individuals and society. Whether through social commentary, inspiration, or reflection, your words can leave a profound mark.

Mentorship: Pass on your wisdom and insights to aspiring writers. Mentorship is a legacy in itself, nurturing the growth of future wordsmiths.

The Path Forward

As we conclude this chapter on embracing the writer's life, envision it as the culmination of your voyage through the world of words. The writer's life is not just a profession; it's a calling, a way of being.

In the chapters that follow, we will delve deeper into the practical aspects of freelance writing, from managing your business and marketing your services to perfecting your craft and achieving your aspirations. Your embrace of the writer's life will be the heartbeat that propels you forward on this extraordinary journey.

Prepare to embark on a journey where the writer's life is not just a profession, but an identity—an exploration of self, an expression of soul, and an enduring legacy in the world of letters. The world of freelance writing is shaped by those who wholeheartedly embrace the writer's life, and you are poised to be among them.

Chapter 19: Perfecting Your Craft

Craftsmanship is the essence of great writing, and in Chapter 19, we embark on a journey to perfect your craft as a freelance writer. It's a quest for excellence, a devotion to storytelling, and an exploration of the myriad techniques and tools that elevate your words from mere text to literary artistry.

The Craft of Writing

Writing is a craft honed through dedication, practice, and an unquenchable thirst for improvement.

The Power of Revision: First drafts are the clay from which masterpieces emerge. Embrace the art of revision. Edit, refine, and sculpt your words until they gleam with brilliance.

Study the Masters: Great writers are often avid readers. Dive into the works of literary giants. Analyze their prose, sentence structure, and storytelling techniques.

Grammar and Style: Mastery of grammar and style is fundamental. Strive for impeccable grammar, but also learn when and how to bend the rules for creative effect.

Character Development

In the realm of fiction, characters are the beating heart of your narrative. Delve deep into their souls and breathe life into them.

Complex Characters: Avoid one-dimensional characters. Give them flaws, fears, and aspirations. Readers should relate to their humanity.

Character Arcs: Characters should evolve throughout the story. Trace their arcs from the first page to the last, revealing transformation and growth.

Show, Don't Tell: Show your characters' emotions and thoughts through actions and dialogue rather than telling readers outright.

Plot and Structure

The architecture of your story determines its impact. Plot and structure are the scaffolding that supports your narrative.

Inciting Incident: Introduce an inciting incident early to hook readers. It's the catalyst that sets your story in motion.

Three-Act Structure: The three-act structure—setup, confrontation, and resolution—provides a solid framework for storytelling.

Conflict and Tension: Conflict is the engine of your plot. Raise stakes, create tension, and challenge your characters to keep readers engaged.

Descriptive Prose

Words are your paintbrush; the canvas is the reader's imagination. Craft vivid and evocative descriptions that transport readers to new worlds.

Sensory Details: Engage the senses. Describe not only how something looks but how it smells, sounds, tastes, and feels.

Metaphors and Similes: Metaphors and similes add depth to descriptions. They create connections between the known and the unknown.

Economy of Words: Use words judiciously. Say more with less. Concise, well-chosen descriptions have a greater impact.

Dialogue and Voice

Dialogue is the lifeblood of characters, and voice is the signature that distinguishes your writing.

Natural Dialogue: Dialogue should sound authentic. Listen to real conversations to capture the rhythm and quirks of speech.

Character Voice: Each character should have a distinct voice. Consider their background, personality, and experiences when crafting their dialogue.

Authorial Voice: Develop your own authorial voice—a unique tone and style that permeate your work and make it instantly recognizable.

Research and Authenticity

Writing often requires research to ensure accuracy and authenticity, whether you're crafting historical fiction or delving into a technical topic.

Primary and Secondary Sources: Consult primary sources when available for firsthand accounts and authenticity. Secondary sources provide context and depth.

Fact-Checking: Fact-check your work rigorously. Inaccuracy can erode trust with readers.

Interviews and Experts: Reach out to experts or conduct interviews to gather firsthand knowledge and insights.

Self-Editing

Editing is an integral part of the writing process. Self-editing hones your work before it reaches a professional editor.

Proofreading: Proofread meticulously for spelling, grammar, and punctuation errors.

Consistency: Ensure consistency in character traits, plot details, and writing style throughout your work.

Beta Readers: Enlist beta readers to provide feedback. Fresh perspectives can uncover blind spots.

The Writing Community

The writing community is a wellspring of support, encouragement, and camaraderie. Engaging with it enriches your writing journey.

Writing Groups: Join writing groups or critique circles to share your work and receive constructive feedback.

Conferences and Workshops: Attend writing conferences and workshops. They offer opportunities to learn, network, and grow.

Online Communities: Explore online writing communities and forums. They provide a virtual space for collaboration and connection.

The Path Forward

As we conclude this chapter on perfecting your craft, envision it as the culmination of your apprenticeship—the moment when your writing reaches new heights of artistry and storytelling.

In the chapters that follow, we will delve deeper into the practical aspects of freelance writing, from thriving in the industry and managing your business to achieving your aspirations and leaving a lasting legacy. Your mastery of the craft will be the cornerstone that elevates your writing to unparalleled heights.

Prepare to embark on a journey where your words are not just sentences but brushstrokes of a literary masterpiece, where your stories resonate deeply with readers, and where your craft as a freelance writer is nothing short of exceptional. The world of freelance writing is shaped by those who perfect their craft, and you are poised to be among them.

Chapter 20: Leaving Your Literary Legacy

As your journey through the realm of freelance writing draws to a close, you stand on the threshold of a remarkable endeavor—leaving behind your literary legacy. Chapter 20 marks the final chapter of this literary odyssey, guiding you through the art of preserving your words, sharing your wisdom, and ensuring your impact endures through time.

The Essence of a Literary Legacy

A literary legacy transcends the written word. It is a testament to your journey, your insights, and your contribution to the world of literature.

Preserving Your Work: To begin, preserve your work diligently. Archive your manuscripts, articles, essays, and published works to safeguard them for posterity.

Copyright Considerations: Understand copyright laws and how they apply to your work. Decide whether you want your work to be protected, or if you're comfortable with it being in the public domain.

Legacy Collections: Consider donating your work to literary archives, libraries, or universities. Your contributions can inspire future generations of writers and scholars.

Sharing Your Wisdom

Sharing your wisdom is an integral part of leaving a literary legacy. It involves imparting knowledge, insights, and experiences gained throughout your writing journey.

Writing Guides: Craft writing guides or books that distill your writing wisdom. These resources can serve as invaluable tools for aspiring writers.

Mentorship Programs: Establish mentorship programs or scholarships to support emerging writers. Your guidance can nurture their growth and potential.

Teaching and Workshops: Continue to teach writing classes or workshops. Sharing your expertise in a structured format helps pass on your knowledge.

Your Personal Narrative

Your personal narrative—your experiences, struggles, and triumphs—adds depth to your legacy. It offers a glimpse into the human side of your writing journey.

Memoirs: Consider writing memoirs or personal essays that chronicle your life as a writer. Share anecdotes and reflections that resonate with readers.

Behind-the-Scenes: Lift the curtain on your creative process. Share stories about how certain works came to be, the challenges you faced, and the inspiration that drove you.

Influence and Impact

The legacy of a writer is often measured by the influence and impact of their words. Consider how you want your work to inspire, educate, or provoke thought.

Social Commentary: Use your writing to address important social issues. Thoughtful commentary can raise awareness and spark conversations.

Inspiration: Inspire others through your stories and experiences. Your journey as a writer can motivate aspiring writers to pursue their own dreams.

Advocacy: Champion causes you are passionate about through your writing. Leverage your influence to drive positive change in society.

Leaving a Digital Footprint

In the digital age, your online presence is a significant part of your literary legacy. Consider how your digital footprint will continue to resonate.

Website and Blog: Maintain your website and blog as repositories of your thoughts, works, and reflections. Ensure they remain accessible and up-to-date.

Social Media: Curate your social media profiles to reflect your literary identity. Engage with your audience, respond to comments, and foster a sense of community.

Legacy Projects

Embark on legacy projects—works specifically designed to encapsulate your literary legacy and the essence of your writing journey.

Anthologies: Curate anthologies of your best works, providing readers with a comprehensive collection of your writing across genres and themes.

Retrospectives: Produce retrospectives or documentaries that delve into your life as a writer. Share interviews, readings, and personal insights.

Letters and Correspondence: Consider publishing your letters and correspondence with fellow writers, editors, and literary figures. These exchanges offer glimpses into your relationships and literary collaborations.

The Path Forward

As we conclude this final chapter on leaving your literary legacy, envision it as the apex of your journey—the culmination of your dedication, creativity, and profound influence.

Your literary legacy is not just a footnote in history; it's a timeless narrative that will inspire, educate, and resonate with generations to come. In the chapters that preceded, we explored the intricacies of freelance writing, from mastering the craft to achieving your aspirations. Now, your legacy takes center stage as a testament to your enduring impact on the world of words.

Prepare to embark on the ultimate chapter—a journey where your words echo through time, where your wisdom becomes a guiding light, and where your legacy as a freelance writer is etched indelibly into the annals of literature. The world of freelance writing is shaped by those who leave a lasting literary legacy, and you are poised to be among them.

Did you love *From Words To Wealth: Mastering Freelance Writing*? Then you should read *The Writer's Odyssey: Crafting Your Literary Legacy, A New Writer's Guide Book*[1] by Richard Krause!

[2]

Embark on an extraordinary journey into the captivating world of writing with " ***The Writer's Odyssey: Crafting Your Literary Legacy, A New Writer's Guide Book*** ". This enlightening guide takes aspiring authors on a voyage through the art and craft of storytelling, from the inception of a writer's dreams to the thrilling adventure of self-expression.

Discover the power of words as you explore the unique tapestry of your imagination. From the first spark of inspiration to the triumph of completing your manuscript, you'll find inspiration and guidance to fuel your creative journey. Uncover the secrets of compelling

---

1. https://books2read.com/u/4A2MVq

2. https://books2read.com/u/4A2MVq

characters, immersive settings, and gripping plots that will keep readers turning pages.

But this book is more than just a guide to the craft; it's a testament to the resilience and determination that define a true writer. Learn how to overcome writer's block, embrace constructive criticism, and persevere through the highs and lows of your writing adventure.

Join a vibrant writing community, connect with fellow authors, and find the support and encouragement you need to flourish. Cultivate your unique voice, explore diverse genres, and celebrate the joy of creative exploration.

Your writing adventure begins here, and every chapter is a milestone in your literary legacy. Whether you dream of becoming a best-selling author, a poet, or simply desire to share your stories with the world, *" The Writer's Odyssey: Crafting Your Literary Legacy, A New Writer's Guide Book "* will be your steadfast companion.

So, new authors, take that first step and let your journey as a writer commence. The blank pages before you are waiting to be transformed into worlds of your creation. Are you ready to craft your literary legacy? It's time to pick up your pen, open your laptop, and begin your *" The Writer's Odyssey: Crafting Your Literary Legacy "*, today. Your words have the power to inspire, entertain, and leave a lasting legacy. Happy writing!

Read more at https://rkrause45.wixsite.com/mysite.

Also by Richard Krause

The Spice Cabinet Apothecary: Natural Health at Your Fingertips"
The Writer's Odyssey: Crafting Your Literary Legacy, A New Writer's
Guide Book
From Words To Wealth: Mastering Freelance Writing
The Morning Elixir of Life: The History and Art of Coffee

Watch for more at https://rkrause45.wixsite.com/mysite.

About the Author

Mr. Krause now resides in the Misty Mountains of West Virginia with his lovely wife of 42 years and their three furry four-legged children, Lexi, Aesop, and Kodi. He also has two adult human children. He is 70-plus years of age and has been writing most of his life.

He spent 60 years home-based in Southwestern Florida. During his military career, he saw 22 foreign countries and all fifty of the United States.

He is a retired government worker, with an extensive background in Environmental Protection. He holds a Degree in Network Engineering and Administration specializing in Computer Security, and has a background in both public and private security.

He has been writing professionally now since 1982. For many years he attempted publishing through mainstream publishing but sadly was overlooked. That is when he decided to go the Indie route. In 2018 he published his first book through KDP, it was *"The Book on Evil, Wicked, Mean & Nasty: A Whimsical Guide to Payback and Revenge"* other titles are *"The Fine Art of Getting Even, a Comical Approach to Revenge"*, *"The Ancient Wisdom of an Old Shadow Warrior"*,*"The Plucking of The Golden Years Goose"*, and *"How to Find Your Way in The Internet Jungle, a Guidebook for Work-At-Homers"*.

He has also created and published five low-content journals, *"My Fishing Log Book"*, *"The Traveling Man's Journal"*, *"My Bedside Dream Journal"*, *"My Writing Idea Book"*, *"The Adventurer's*

Notebook" all of which are available on that big box store on the Internet.

Besides reading and writing he is an enthusiastic fisherman, his hobbies are, building and painting 54mm military figures, cutting and polishing semi-precious gemstones, creating unique hand-crafted jewelry, and the restoration of vintage and antique weapons.

He has studied several forms of oriental martial arts for over 50 years. But sadly due to health concerns is no longer able to practice.

Read more at https://rkrause45.wixsite.com/mysite.

www.ingramcontent.com/pod-product-compliance
Lightning Source LLC
Chambersburg PA
CBHW050753160726
48004CB00002B/544